WHY

SHOULD

I GO

TO

CHURCH?

* * *

"WHY SHOULD
I GO TO CHURCH?
WHY CAN'T I JUST
DO DEVOTIONS
ON MY OWN?"

* * *

nothing will do except to join with fellow Christians in praise of our great God. Jesus promised: "For where two or three are gathered in my name, there am I among them" (Matthew 18:20). God is glorified when Christians speak of his greatness with each other, and he is pleased to be in our midst.

3. PERSONAL GROWTH

Just as individual Bible study and prayer are vital to a Christian's spiritual growth, so is consistent contact with other Christians. God commands us to "consider how to stir up one another to love and good works, not neglecting to meet together . . . " (Hebrews 10:24–25). Meeting regularly with other Christians is an opportunity to be encouraged in your daily walk with Christ, to receive godly advice in areas of difficulty in your life, and to be challenged by the example of more mature Christians.

4. MINISTRY

Paul wrote that God gave us "shepherds and teachers, to equip the saints for the work of ministry, for building up the body of Christ" (Ephesians 4:11–12). Attending church allows us to receive the instruction of trained pastors and teachers, helping us minister to the world and to other Christians.

Along with communicating the gospel to the unsaved through actions and words, Christians have a responsibility to minister to other members of the body of Christ: "Therefore encourage one another and build one another up" (1 Thessalonians 5:11). Being in regular contact with other Christians in church gives you numerous opportunities to offer a word of encouragement, a listening ear, a helping hand, or to receive these things in your moment of need.

HOW TO CHOOSE A CHURCH

Consider the following questions as you visit new churches:

1. Does the church base its teachings on the Bible? Do they teach the fundamentals of the gospel?

2. Is there a sense of community? Are the people friendly? Would you like to get to know the people that you meet there?

3. Does the church have programs that meet your family's needs? Are there classes for your children? Is there a group for your teenager to get involved in?

4. Does the church support missions and encourage evangelism? Does it provide opportunities for outreach?

Feel free to visit several different churches before making a decision. Meet some of the people and talk to the pastor. Ask questions. Don't forget to pick up a church brochure with

1. FELLOWSHIP

Regular church attendance allows a Christian to become part of a church family—a community of brothers and sisters in Christ who share true concern for one another. Paul described this kind of fellowship in his letter to the Corinthians: "If one member suffers, all suffer together; if one member is honored, all rejoice together" (1 Corinthians 12:26). When we care for our fellow Christians in this way, not only do we enjoy the security of belonging to a spiritual family, but we also glorify God by revealing his character to the world.

2. CORPORATE WORSHIP

When God rescued King David from his enemies, David couldn't keep his praise to himself. He cried out, "Oh, magnify the LORD with me, and let us exalt his name together!" (Psalm 34:3). Even Christ, in the darkest hours of his life, asked three of his closest friends to "watch and pray" with him (Matthew 26:41). Private devotion pleases God, but at times,

GOOD QUESTION!

It's true that God values personal devotions. In fact, he even commands us to "pray without ceasing" (1 Thessalonians 5:17). But "going to church" is about more than personal devotion. For Christians, going to church is the gathering together of a family, or as the apostle Paul described it, uniting the members of a body:

"For as in one body we have many members, and the members do not all have the same function, so we, though many, are one body in Christ, and individually members one of another." (Romans 12:4–5)

Every Christian is a member of the body of Christ, and every member has unique talents and insights. Sharing these gifts with each other as a unified body strengthens us in our common task of glorifying God. In the joy of true community you will experience:

a listing of services and programs, as well as a mission statement. Discuss the experience with your family and visit again if you need to. Pray that you may discern God's will for your family's spiritual growth.

ISBN 978-1-6821-6375-7

www.goodnewstracts.org